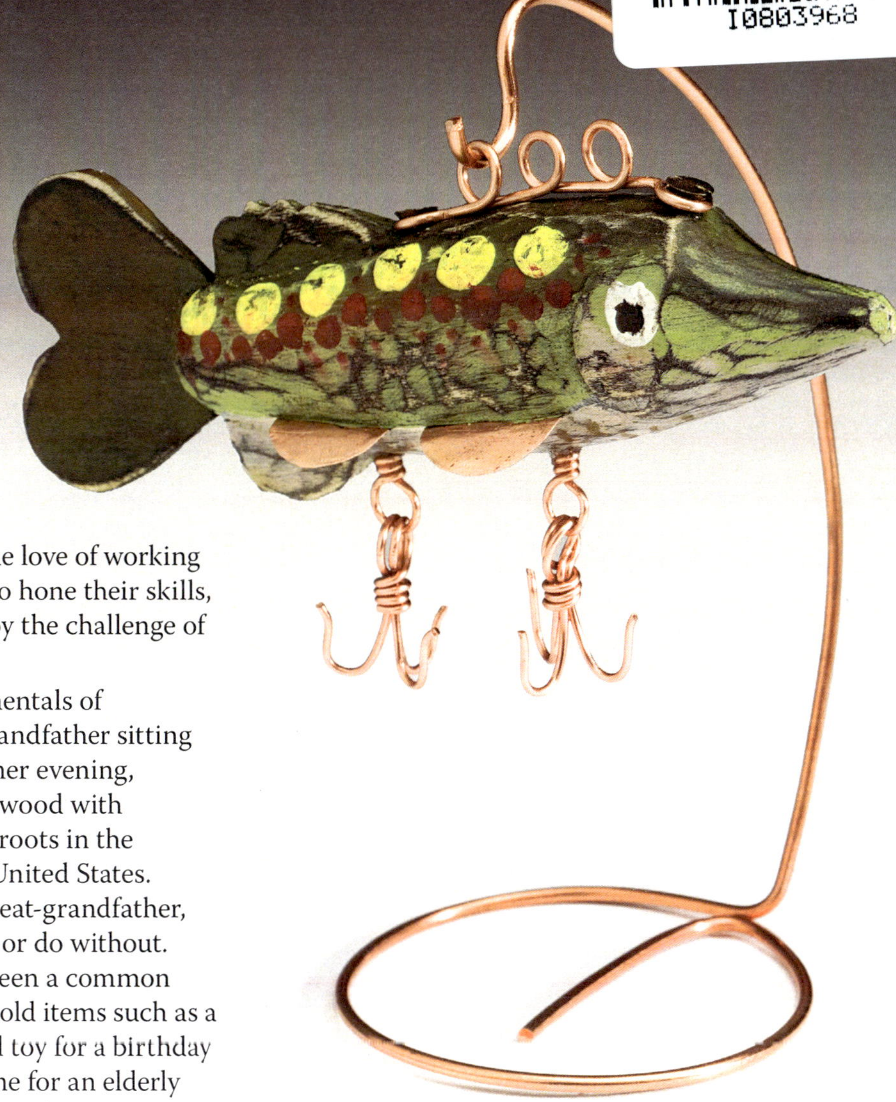

For me, whittling is individually expressive and uniquely creative—a perfect opportunity for beginning carvers to learn the love of working wood, for intermediate carvers to hone their skills, and for advanced carvers to enjoy the challenge of returning to one-knife work.

When I think of the fundamentals of whittling, I imagine my great-grandfather sitting on the back steps on a hot summer evening, quietly working a small piece of wood with his pocketknife. Our family has roots in the Appalachian Mountains of the United States. Money was often tight for my great-grandfather, so he learned to make it himself or do without. For him, whittling would have been a common practice—creating small household items such as a stopper for a glass bottle, a small toy for a birthday present, or a walking stick or cane for an elderly relative. My great-granddad did not have access to the variety of woodcarving gouges, chisels, and skews we have today, but he had a pocketknife and that's all he needed to whittle.

Over time, whittlers added a little artistic expression to those household items. Bottle stoppers, meant to seal vinegar or oil in a glass container, became caricatures of animal or human heads. Canes were decorated with twisting snakes, fanciful creatures, and geometric patterns. Walking sticks turned into story sticks carved with lettering to record important events in the cane owner's life. Many historic story sticks date from the American Civil War and record the dates and names of the battles soldiers fought. Tramps carved small animals as toys and traded them to young mothers for a meal. Whittling fulfilled the daily needs of the carver's family, but whittlers could not resist adding a little bit of art to that necessity.

Originally, fish lures like the one we'll be making were necessary tools to put food on the table. We'll be using simple shapes, a few carved details, a bit of wood or copper for fins, and one knife to carve an artistic folk-art-style fishing lure. You'll also learn how to expand on the simple one-knife techniques to create other basic lure shapes. Every tool and supply is available at your local arts and crafts store, and you may already have many of them at hand.

I have tried to show every step along the path to creating this folk-art fishing lure. Every time I change the area that I am carving, change the basic shape of the wood blank, or take a new step in adding fins, copper, and creating hooks, I have shown you that step through photos. This book will guide you in your first cuts and show you how simple, easy, and creative whittling wood can be.

CHAPTER 1

Carving Safely

Regardless of what you plan to carve, keep in mind a few basic safety concerns. You are using a sharp blade, and if the knife is sharp enough to cut wood, it is sharp enough to cut your skin. We'll learn how to prevent injuries and how to make a few basic cuts, and then, it will be time to start whittling.

Wear a thumb guard.

A thumb guard protects your thumb from the sharp edge. This is especially helpful when making a paring cut. To perform a paring cut, which is one of the basic cuts of whittling, anchor the thumb of your knife-holding hand on the blank and tighten your fist to draw the knife through the wood, similar to the motion you make when peeling a potato.

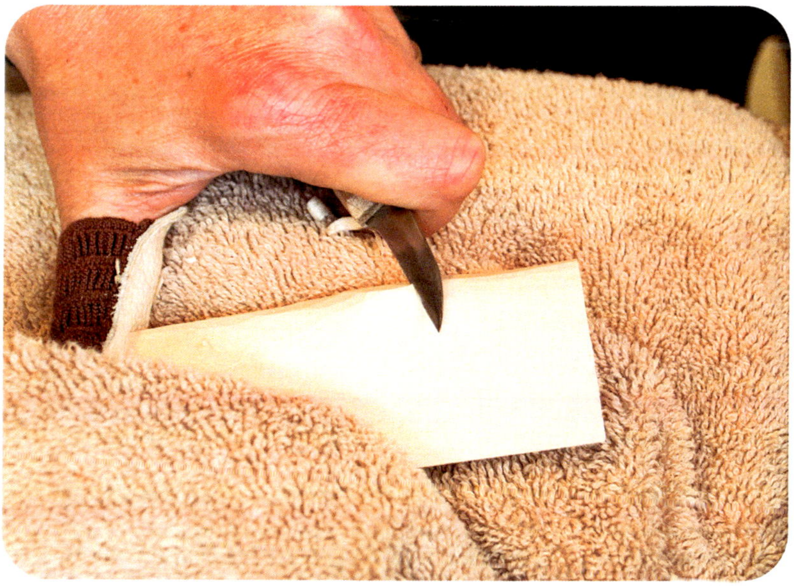

Protect your holding hand.

Some carvers wear a protective glove on the hand they use to hold the blank. I use a heavy terrycloth towel to protect my holding hand from cuts. I usually carve with the wood in my lap and use the towel not only for protection, but also to catch the chips, making it easy to clean up after a carving session.

Tune up your knife.

Begin any carving session by ensuring that you have a sharp knife. I use a coarse 600- to 800-grit stone, a fine 2000- to 6000-grit stone, a leather strop, and honing compound. While carving, stop often and hone, or strop, your knife on the leather strop to keep the edge as sharp as possible. A dull knife is a dangerous knife because you need to apply more pressure to make the cut, and you sacrifice control as you apply additional pressure.

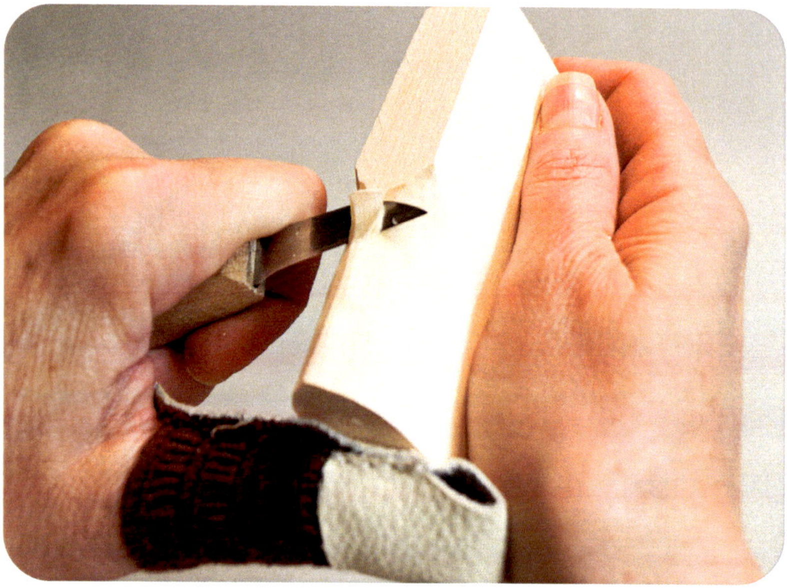

Watch where the blade could go.

A glove and thumb guard will slow down a blade, but they may not totally stop a cut. Position your fingers and hands so that if the blade slips, there is nothing for it to cut. I position my thumb lower on the blank so that if the wood splits or I lose control as I make a paring cut, the knife won't cut my thumb.

Practice the forward pushing cut.

This cut is useful to remove wood quickly. Position the thumb of your knife-holding hand on the back of the blade. Position the thumb of your wood-holding hand on the back of your other thumb and push the knife through the wood. Notice that the holding hand grips the wood below the area where the cutting stroke will end.

For more on basic whittling cuts and sharpening, visit www.WoodcarvingIllustrated.com.

materials & tools

MATERIALS:

- Basswood:
  - Vintage gar, speckled minnow, large mouth bass, sunny: 7/8" x 1 1/2" x 4" (22mm x 38mm x 102mm)
  - Green gar, spotted minnow, gray mouse: 7/8" x 7/8" x 4" (22mm x 22mm x 102mm)
  - Copper-finned blue gill: 7/8" x 1 1/2" x 2" (22mm x 38mm x 51mm)
  - Wooden fins: 3/16" x 3" x 3" (5mm x 76mm x 76mm)
  - Bobber: 7/8" x 7/8" x 2" (22mm x 22mm x 51mm)
- Dowel (bobber): 3/16"-diameter x 10"-long (5mm x 254mm)
- Copy of pattern
- Thin cardboard, such as a cereal box
- Spray adhesive or double-sided tape
- Brown paper bag
- Sandpaper: 220-grit
- Cyanoacrylate (CA) glue or wood glue
- Thin copper sheet
- Small brass screws: 1/4" (6mm) long
- Copper wire: 12- and 18-gauge
- Acrylic paints: black, burnt sienna, titanium white, medium green, pale yellow, red
- Paper towels
- Permanent markers: metallic gold or silver, black, red
- Acrylic spray sealer: high-gloss
- Mason's line or other heavy cord

TOOLS:

- Carving knife or pocketknife
- Thumb guard
- Carving glove and/or terrycloth towel
- Leather strop and honing compound
- Pencil with a new eraser
- Penny or other 3/4" (19mm)-diameter coin
- Craft scissors
- Old toothbrush
- Tape or rubber bands (optional)
- Wire cutters
- Pliers: flat-nose, round-nose
- 2" (76mm)-diameter vitamin or medicine bottle (display stand)
- Assorted small paintbrushes
- Paint palette
- Drill with drill bits: 1/16" (2mm)-, 1/4" (6mm)-diameter
- Lint-free cloth
- Screwdriver

The author used these products for the project. Substitute your choice of brands, tools, and materials as desired.

CHAPTER 2

Carving the Lure

Creating the basic shape of the lure's body is the first step in carving this fish lure. Each fish species has a basic body profile that is recognizable to the fish that prey upon that species. Even though you may not be carving a working fishing lure, it will look more realistic and authentic if you stay with an identifiable body shape.

With its long thin body, downward-cupped head, and long narrow mouth area, this lure looks like a gar. A blue gill or sunfish has a small, round, compact body that is about as long as it is tall. Bottom feeders, such as catfish, often have an almost straight belly line with a large head that curves down toward the creek bed. A large, wide-open mouth area on a lure suggests a bass.

If this is your first project as a new woodcarver, I strongly suggest you use basswood for the lure. Although classified as a hardwood, basswood is soft and easy to carve. Basswood has a tight fine grain and a clean light color that accepts paint well. As your carving skills grow, you can try soft maple, cedar, black walnut, or even sugar pine for lure blanks. Cut the carving blank to size, aligning the grain with the length of the block.

DO NOT carve balsa wood, even though it is readily available at arts and crafts stores. Balsa is an extremely soft wood. When carving against the grain, you are just as likely to dent balsa as to cut it, which makes it difficult to carve.

You can use a carving knife or pocketknife to carve this project. For tips on choosing a knife and information about different types of pocketknives, see www.WoodcarvingIllustrated.com.

TIPS **USING A CENTERLINE**

Most things in nature are symmetrical, which means the two halves are mirror images of each other. If you divide the lure down the middle (along the back and belly), both halves should be mirror images of each other. To keep things in proportion and symmetrical, mark this dividing line, which is called a centerline, and use it as a reference as you shape the piece.

CARVING: PREPARING THE BLANK

1 **Remove the sharp corners from the long sides.** The ultimate goal is a fish shape with a rounded body. Carve away all of the sharp edges of the blank. Begin by carving away the edges along the long sides of the blank. As you work away from those crisp edges, the blank will begin to gently roll toward the centerline of the wood. Use a paring cut or a forward push cut, depending on the grain direction.

2 **Make small controlled cuts.** Keep the angle between the knife blade and the wood low. The goal is to remove small slivers of wood. Increasing the angle between the blade and the wood lets you remove wood faster, but with less control. A low angle and thin slivers are the keys to controlling your cuts.

3 **Finish removing the corners from the blank.** When you have removed all of the long-side corners, begin carving away the corners on the short sides. Begin at the edge of the blank and slowly work back to the centerline. Keep carving until the blank is pillow shaped and the entire wood surface is lightly carved.

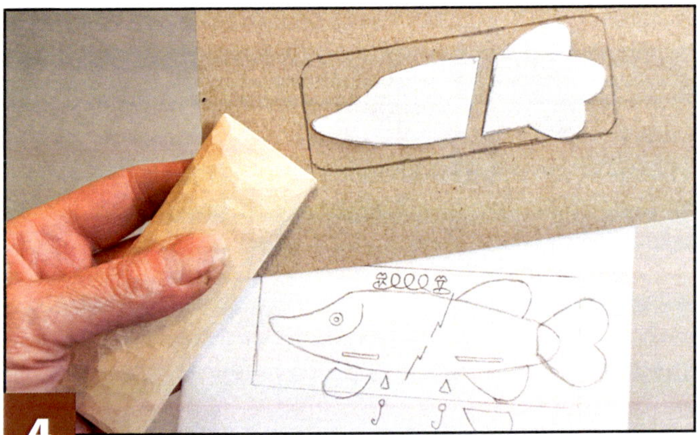

4 **Create a template.** Make a copy of the pattern on page 15. Cut around the perimeter of the copy. Trace the perimeter of the blank onto a piece of thin cardboard, such as a cereal box. Align the snout and tail with the outside edges of the rectangle. If the pattern is too big or small, adjust the size per the Tip at left. Apply spray adhesive or double-sided tape to the back of the paper pattern and adhere it to the cardboard. Cut around the pattern attached to the cardboard to create a template.

TIPS ADJUSTING PATTERN SIZE

If your wood blank is slightly larger or smaller than your decoy pattern, you can easily adjust the pattern length. First, trace the perimeter of the blank onto lightweight cardboard. Then, cut the paper pattern diagonally through the center. Align the front and back of the pattern to the edges of the box; the pieces will overlap or gap, depending on the size of the blank. Adhere the pattern to the cardboard. If necessary, draw guidelines to connect the two halves. See Step 4.

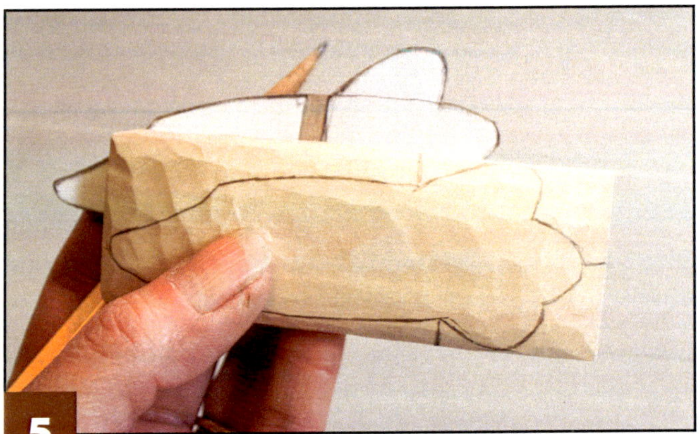

5 **Trace the pattern onto the blank.** Place the template onto the wide side of the blank and trace along the edge of the template with a pencil. Mark the location of the front of each fin and the center of the tail onto the sides of the blank. Use those marks to align the template on the opposite side of the blank. You can use the template to create many different lures with different paint schemes or hardware.

CARVING: ROUGHING OUT THE BODY

6 **Begin removing the excess wood from the back of the lure.** Working along the top edge of the lure's back, begin removing the excess wood above the pattern outline. In these steps, carve with the grain of the wood (See Tip).

TIPS DEFINITION: GRAIN

Wood contains long tubular fibers, called grain, that run vertical to the tree's growth. Cutting with the grain runs the sharp edge along those fibers. This makes the cuts easy, and requires minimal pressure to move the knife through the wood.

Working with end grain, or across the grain, means you are cutting across the tubular fibers of the wood. Instead of the cutting edge sliding between those long fibers, it is now cutting every fiber. When carving the end grain, you need to apply more pressure and take smaller cuts to maintain control.

7 **Continue removing the excess wood.** Make several small cuts in an area and then remove them as a larger group. The work of removing the waste wood leaves a square edge above the pattern line. This area will be rounded in later steps. Notice I have not carved the angle between the fin and body down to the pattern line yet.

CARVING: ROUGHING OUT THE HEAD

8 **Rough out the head.** Carefully remove the waste wood on both sides of the head. Redraw the centerline as needed to keep the head symmetrical. The goal is to create a wedge shape with a high point on the centerline of the back.

9 **Draw in the top of the head.** The intersection between the back and head is curved in this lure. Use a pencil to draw a curved line at this intersection line.

10 **Finish roughing out the head.** Hold the knife so there is a shallow angle between the blade and the blank. Carefully shave down the top of the head along the pencil line using a forward pushing cut. End the cuts in the snout area.

CARVING: ROUGHING OUT THE BELLY

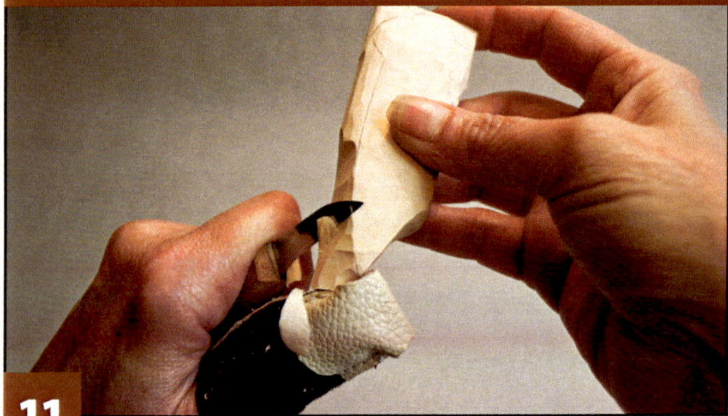

11 **Begin carving the bottom of the lure.** Remove the excess wood from under the head. Use a paring cut, cutting with the grain of the wood.

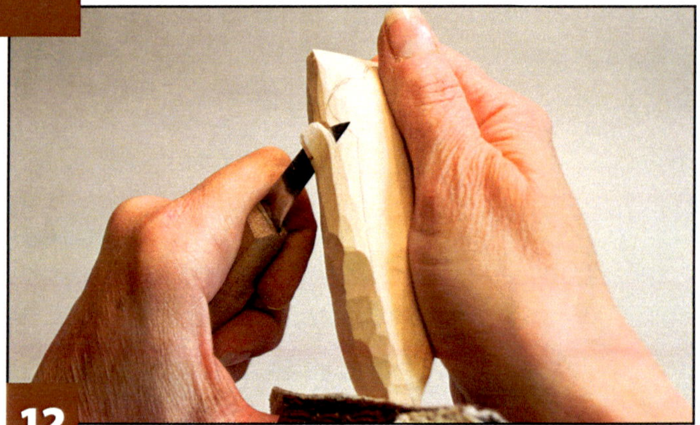

12 **Finish roughing out the lure's belly.** To remove a thicker sliver of wood, increase the angle between the knife and the blank. As you gain confidence in your carving ability, experiment with changing the angle between the knife and the blank to see how you can make different cuts.

CARVING: ROUGHING OUT THE TAIL AREA

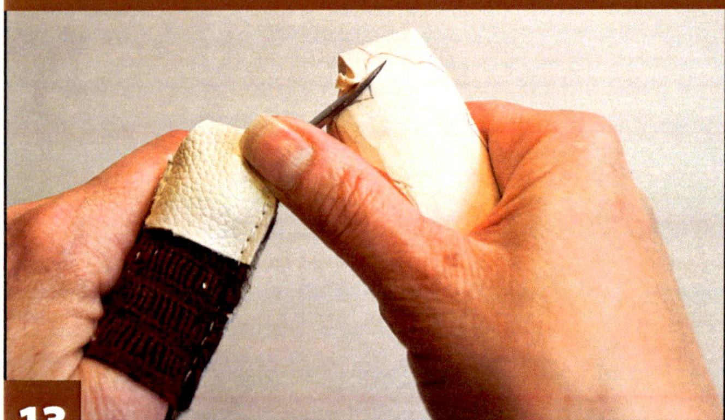

13 **Remove the excess wood around the top of the tail area.** Due to the tight curves on the tail, you need to make small cuts and carefully roll the edge of the knife outward to keep from cutting too deeply.

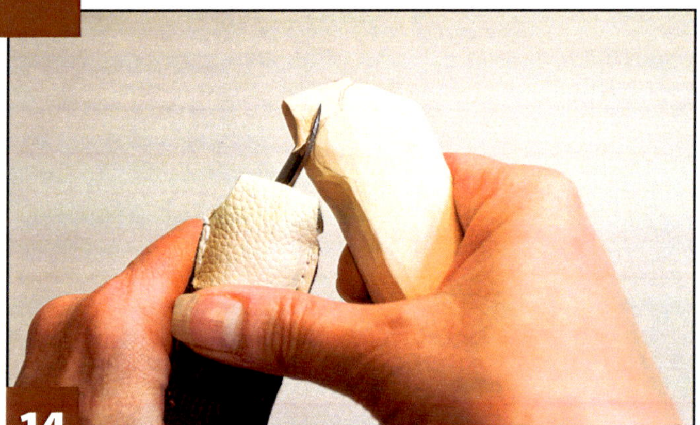

14 **Remove the excess wood from the bottom of the tail area.** Use the same technique explained in Step 13.

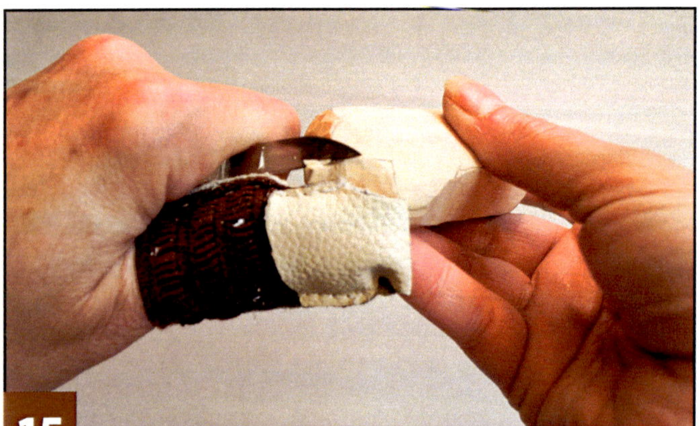

15 **Finish roughing out the tail area.** Remove the remaining small point of wood left in the tail area. Because you are cutting across the end grain, make small cuts to maintain control while removing the excess wood in this area.

CARVING: REFINING THE TAIL AREA

16 **Cut the angle between the bottom fin and the tail area.** First, cut along one side of the angle with the knife, stopping at the point of the angle. Don't try to cut through the whole width of the blank; just concentrate on cutting the angle on one side.

17 **Finish cutting the angle.** Cut in from the opposite direction to meet the first cut at the point of the angle. Remove the waste wood, leaving a sharply angled intersection between the bottom fin and the tail area. You may need to repeat Steps 16 and 17 more than once to remove the waste wood.

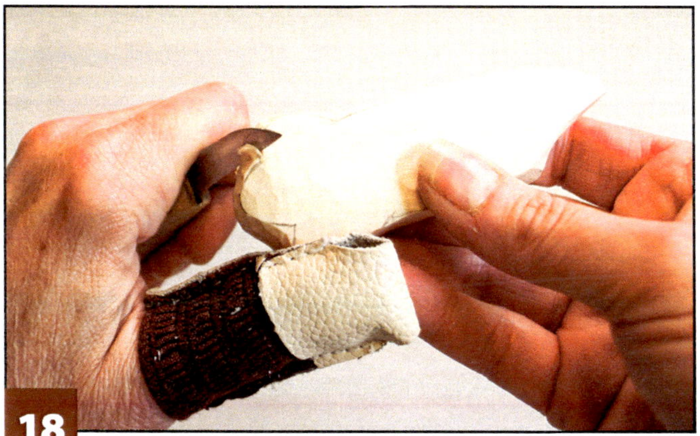

18 **Cut the other side of the angle.** Turn the blank over and repeat Steps 16 and 17 to create the sharply pointed angle between the tail area and the bottom fin on the other side. The angle should now reach across the tail area.

19 **Refine the area where the bottom fin meets the tail area.** Round the cuts carefully to finish shaping the intersection between the fin and tail area, and to remove any remaining waste. Repeat Steps 16 through 19 to cut the angle between the top fin and the tail area.

CARVING: SHAPING THE FINS

20 **Shape the fronts of the fins.** The front edges of the fins are long with a more gradual angle than at the backs of the fins where they meet the tail. Use longer cutting strokes to shape the fronts of the fins. Make the first cut along the top fin and stop at the body.

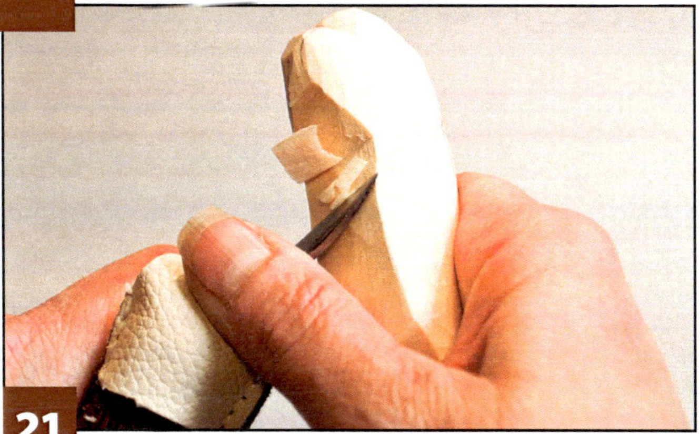

21 **Finish shaping the front of the top fin.** Make a long thin slice across the back up to the cut you made in Step 20 to help separate the top fin from the back.

CARVING: SHAPING THE FINS

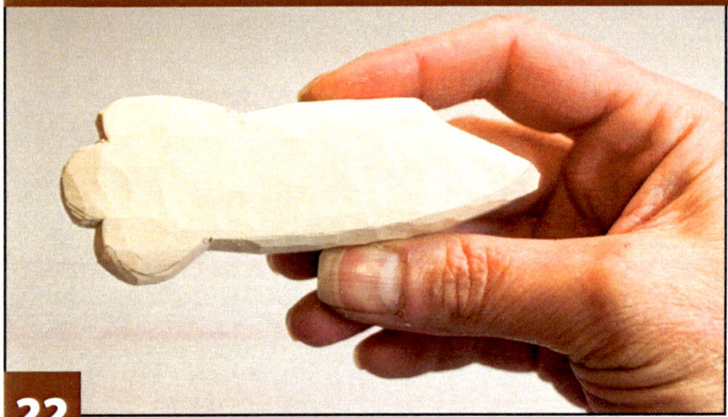

22 **Shape the front of the bottom fin.** Repeat Steps 20 and 21 to cut the angle between the bottom fin and the belly. All of the waste wood should be removed, leaving crisp angles for the fin and body joints, a curved body and head joint, and a curved pointed face area.

23 **Mark the width of the fins.** Make two pencil marks along the center of the fins approximately $1/8$" (3mm) apart. This will be the finished width of the fins.

24 **Mark the fin joints.** Using a pencil, mark the side joints between the fish body and fins on both sides of the lure.

25 **Begin shaping the top and bottom fins.** Use the tip of the knife to make a shallow cut along the pencil lines where the fins meet the body. Apply smooth even pressure as you pull the tip of the knife along the lines. This cut is called a stop cut.

26 **Refine the thickness of the fins.** Move to the top of the fin and carefully slice along the fin up to the stop cut made in Step 25. This process is similar to the technique used to shape the intersection between the fins and the body. This technique allows you to remove the excess wood around the fin without damaging the lure's body.

27 **Finish refining the fins.** Continue making stop cuts and slicing cuts as explained in Steps 25 and 26 until you reach the pencil lines marking the thickness of the fins. Leave a little extra wood around the pencil lines so you can shape the lure as the carving develops. You can always carve away a little excess wood, but you can't put wood back once it is removed. Repeat Steps 25 through 27 on both sides of the top and bottom fins.

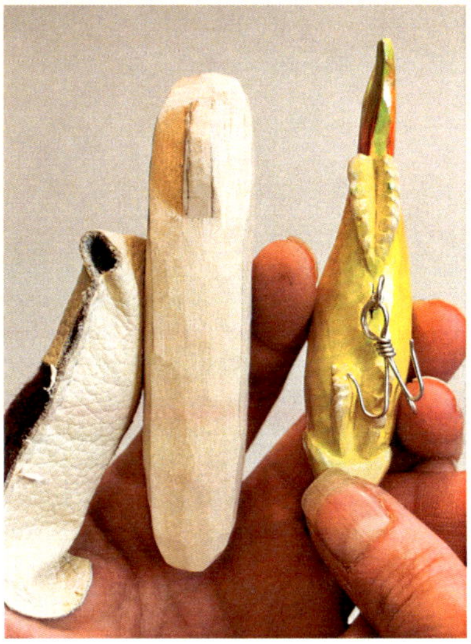

Fancy Fins

This lure's fins are straight, but as you grow more confident, you can easily add a curved fin or even a double fin. To make a curved fin, draw a curved line when marking the thickness of the fin. To make a double fin, mark the width of the flared fins. Carve away the excess wood from around the fins. Angle the tip of the knife inward and make a cut toward the center of the double fin from one side. Flip the carving around and carve in toward the center from the other side to make a V-shaped cut separating the double fins.

CARVING: SHAPING THE BODY

28 **Draw the shape of the body.** Minnows are thin from side to side. The head and tail areas are usually thinner than the chest and belly. Draw a long V on the front and back of the lure to represent the head and tail area.

29 **Begin shaping the lure's body.** Start on one edge and carve away the excess wood outside the V-lines drawn in Step 28. As you make the cuts, carefully round the area toward the centerline. Taper the sides of the body back toward the tail area.

TIPS TIME TO STROP

A dull knife requires you to push harder and leaves behind small fine lines on the wood as you make a cut. Hone the knife a few times on a leather strop to restore the sharp edge.

30 **Finish rough-shaping the body.** Continue tapering the front and back of the body toward the head or tail area, following the V-lines sketched in Step 28.

CARVING: REFINING THE BODY

31 **Refine the back of the body.** The rough-shaping process produces sharp edges. Position the knife so the angle between the blade and the lure is shallow, and carve thin slices of wood as you remove the sharp corners and round the belly. Remove the large marks left by the deeper cutting strokes.

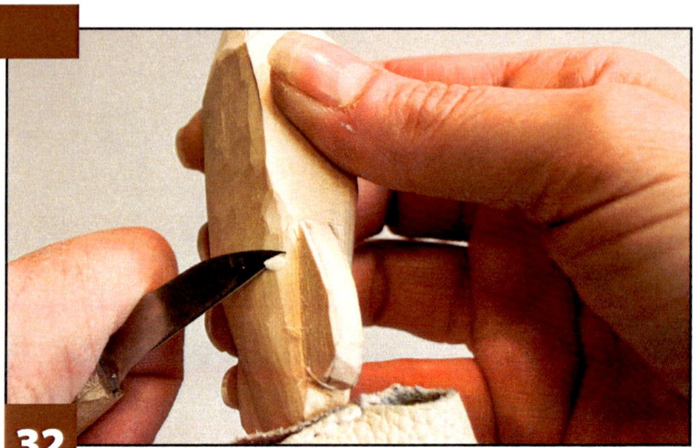

32 **Continue refining the body.** Position the knife on the highest point along the sides and carve to the lowest point. Work from the high point of the back to the low point at the tail. Round the body into a slightly flattened barrel shape. Round the body toward the centerline of the belly and the back.

CARVING: REFINING THE FACE

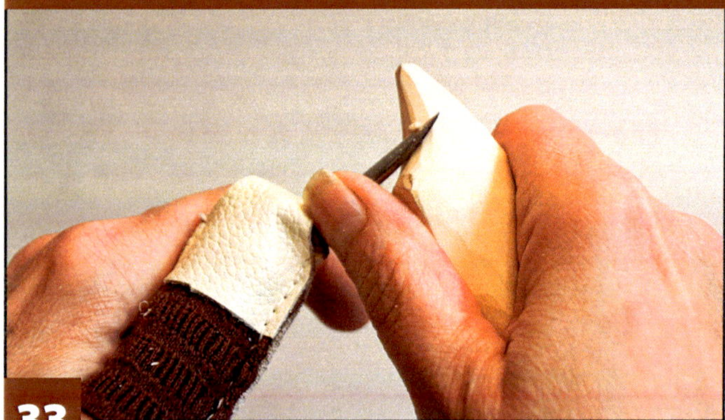

33 **Refine the face.** Shape and curve the edges of the face and snout. Round the sharp corners of the lower jaw. Work from the sharp outer corners toward the centerline of the bottom jaw. Round the mouth area.

34 **Refine the intersection of the head and back.** Cut down at an angle at the intersection of the back and head to remove the sharp edge. Shape the area where the head joins the body.

35 **Create a smooth transition between the back and head.** Make short shallow cuts to create a gentle roll from the back down to the head. The goal is to give the back a rounded torpedo shape with no sharp angles.

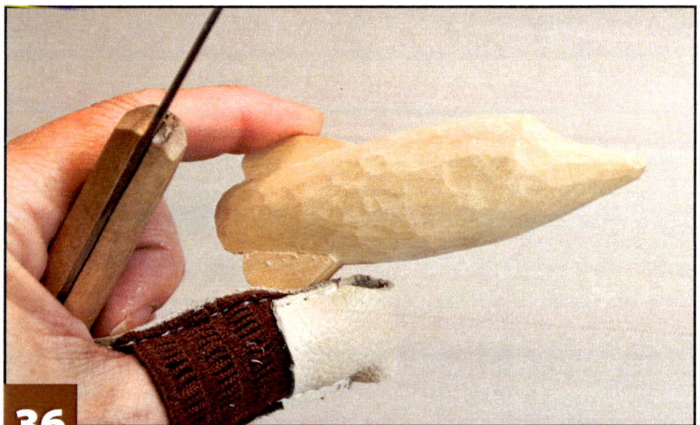

36 **Finish shaping the lure.** Round the belly using the techniques explained in Step 31 and 32. Remove any sharp corners and round the belly toward the centerline.

CARVING: ADDING THE FIN DETAILS

37 **Thin the fins.** Fins are thick at the base where they attach to the body, but thin and pointed at the edges. Make shallow cuts to taper the top and bottom fins to a thin point along the outer edges. This gives the fins a triangular shape when viewed from the front or back.

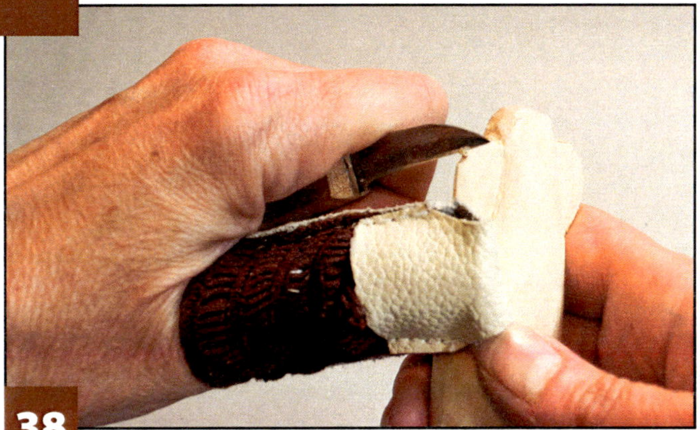

38 **Carve notches into the edge of the top fin.** Make a cut from one side and then carve up to the cut from the other side to remove a wedge-shaped chip from the edge of the fin. I remove three wedges from random areas on the top fin. Carve similar wedges from the bottom fin if you like.

39 **Refine the intersections between the fins and the body.** Hold the knife so there is a very shallow angle between the blade and the fin. Make a thin slice up to the intersection point. Then, position the knife so there is a very shallow angle between the blade and the body. Slice up to the intersection point to clean up the intersection. Repeat for all intersections.

40 **Finish the joints between the fins and the body.** Turn the knife around and press the blunt edge (the edge opposite the cutting edge) across the joint line. Called "burnishing," this technique presses any loose or stray fibers back into position. Burnish all of the joints.

41 **Finish carving the fins.** The triangular shape of the fins creates harsh edges that need to be rounded. Remove the sharp corners from the front and back edges of the fins.

CARVING: ADDING THE FINAL DETAILS

42 **Prepare to add the tail.** Roll the edges of the tail area using shallow shaving cuts. Keep the general barrel shape of the body, but begin tapering the tail area to prepare for the tail, which will be carved separately and glued on later.

43 **Buff the carving.** Crumple a small piece of brown paper bag and rub it against the carving. The paper bag is abrasive enough to remove any stray wood fibers, accumulated dirt, or pencil marks without sanding off any of the small knife-cut planes that mark the lure as a handcarved project.

44 **Draw the gills onto the sides of the face.** Position a penny on the side of the face so the edge lines up with the gill line shown on the pattern. Trace a half-circle around the edge of the penny to represent the gills. Repeat on the other side.

45 **Extend the gill lines under the head area.** Some minnows have long gill lines that almost touch the tip of the mouth. Use the pattern as a guide.

46 **Make a stop cut along the gill lines.** Use the point of the knife to make thin shallow cuts along the gill lines.

47 **Finish carving the gills.** Move the knife blade slightly away from the gill line and cut up to the stop cut made in Step 46. This relief cut releases a chip of wood, resulting in a shallow groove along the gill line. Repeat on the other side.

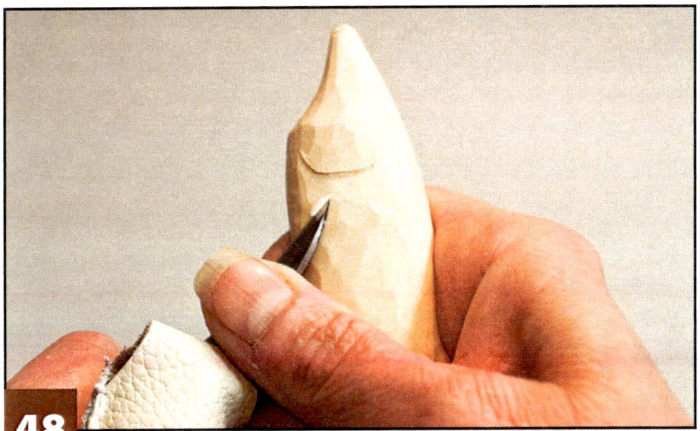

48 **Refine the gills.** Carefully taper the body down into the gill grooves using thin shaving cuts. Do not make the grooves any deeper. The goal is to make the body flow down into the gill grooves.

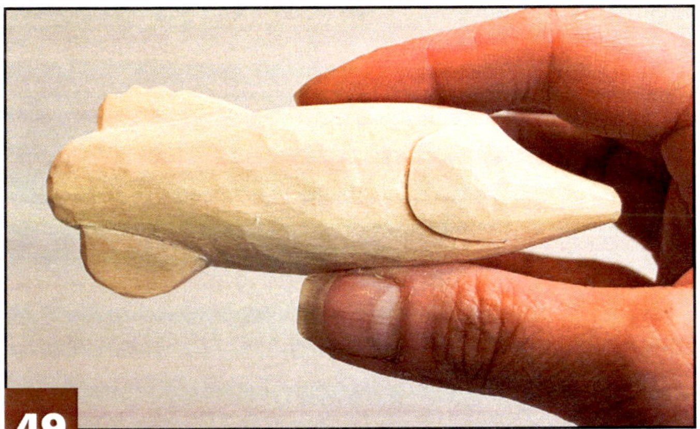

49 **Clean up the carving.** Erase any pencil lines that remain and buff the carving with a crumpled paper bag to smooth any remaining loose fibers. The visible knife cuts are a common surface finish for a whittling project. If you prefer, you can go over the lure with fine shaving cuts to produce a more refined surface.

TIPS **ADD TEXTURE TO THE FINS OR TAIL**

To add more detail to the fins and tail, use the techniques explained in Steps 46 and 47 to carve thin lines and barbs onto the fins and tail.

Vintage gar pattern

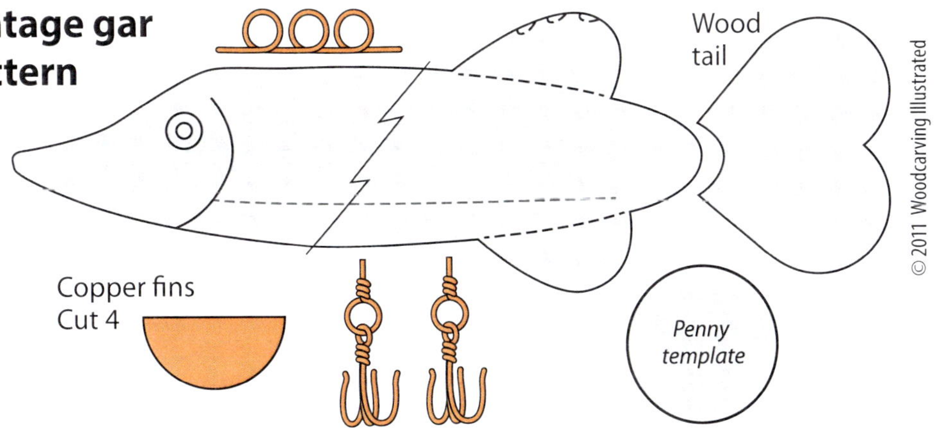

CHAPTER 3

Adding the Tail and Copper Fins

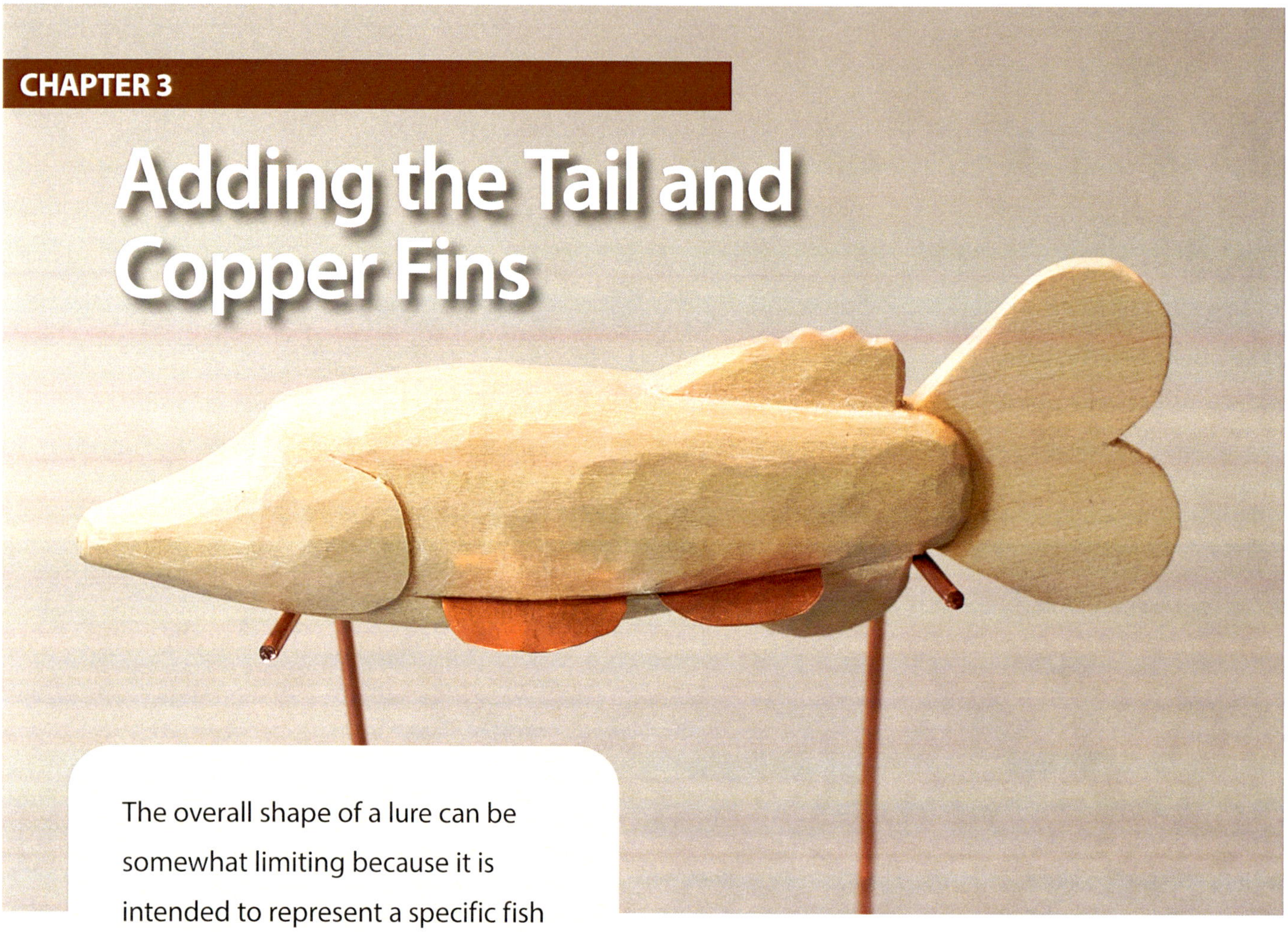

The overall shape of a lure can be somewhat limiting because it is intended to represent a specific fish species, and if carved as a working lure, designed to attract predator fish. However, you can personalize the fins and tail by carving separate elements and gluing them to the lure, or by using copper or thin metal to create the remaining fins.

For this lure, I carve the tail from a separate piece of wood and glue it into a channel carved on the back of the body. I use half circles cut from a sheet of copper for the side fins, which guide the lure's movement through the water.

You can use all carved fins, as shown in the large-mouth bass or speckled minnow samples, all copper fins, as shown in the bluegill, all added-wood fins, as shown in the spotted minnow, or any combination of the three. Some vintage lures eliminate the top, bottom, and side fins, focusing instead on just the body and tail.

My great-grandfather might have cut fins from a tin can or an old automobile license plate. Often pennies were hammered to slightly flatten them, and then cut in half with tin snips to create two side fins. I use pennies as a template to trace small, round, easy-to-cut shapes on copper sheeting.

Other common household items can adorn a fish lure. Scrap leather or rubber salvaged from old tire inner tubes can take the place of copper sheeting to create fins. This is an area where every carver can think outside the box to create unique lures.

TAIL AND FINS: SHAPING THE TAIL

1

Draw the tail onto the blank. Position a penny about ½" (13mm) from the edge of a 3/16" (5mm)-thick blank. Trace two half-circles that touch in the center. Extend the lines down to the edge of the blank to create a heart shape with an open bottom.

2

Rough out the tail. Use a knife to remove the excess wood from around the pencil lines drawn in Step 1. Leave the triangular wedge of wood at the top of the heart for last.

3

Shape the top of the heart. This area is end grain, which can be more difficult to carve. Make small cuts to make sure you retain control.

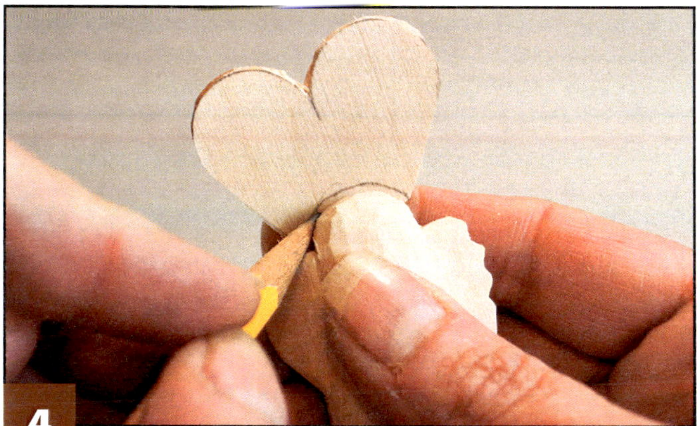

4

Trace the shape of the body onto the tail. Hold the tail blank behind the lure's back end. Using a pencil, trace the lure's back-end profile onto the tail.

5

Match the shape of the tail to the body. Carve away the excess wood at the bottom of the heart shape. Leave about ⅛" (3mm) of wood outside the pencil line. This excess wood will be glued into a groove carved in the lure's back end.

6 **Refine the tail.** Smooth and round the outside edges of the tail slightly with 220-grit sandpaper.

TAIL AND FINS: REFINING THE TAIL'S FIT

7 **Mark the thickness of the tail onto the lure.** Hold the tail in place on the lure and mark the outside edges of the tail onto the back end of the lure blank. These lines mark the width of the groove needed to accommodate the tail.

8 **Make a stop cut along the edges of the tail groove.** Use the tip of the knife to cut long straight lines into the tail on the inside of the pencil lines. Cut the lines from the intersection of the top fin and the body down to the intersection of the bottom fin and the body.

9 **Begin carving the groove for the tail.** Angle your knife slightly and cut from the center of the groove toward the stop cut made in Step 8. This removes a thin sliver of wood. Make the same cut on both sides of the tail to hollow the groove.

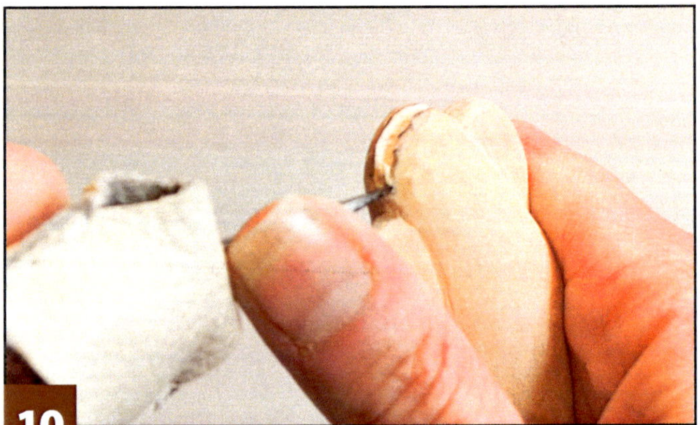

10 **Continue carving the groove for the tail.** Carefully angle your knife more and carve up to the grooves carved in Step 9 until you can flatten the bottom of the groove. Make a stop cut at the ends of the groove and carve up to the stop cut to finish carving the groove.

11 **Refine the groove.** Use 220-grit sandpaper to remove any remaining slivers or fibers of wood in the tail groove. Remove any sanding dust using an old toothbrush or paintbrush.

12 **Test the fit of the tail.** Position the tail in the groove and make sure it fits tightly. The tighter the tail fits in the groove, the stronger the glue joint will be. It is easier to adjust the shape of the tail than it is to adjust the shape of the groove. Fine-tune the tail by carving away small amounts of wood until you get a tight fit.

TAIL AND FINS: ATTACHING THE TAIL

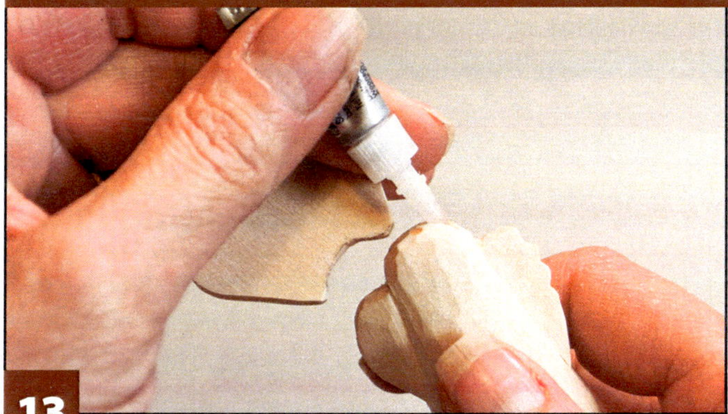

13 **Attach the tail to the body.** When you are satisfied with the fit, attach the tail to the body with cyanoacrylate (CA) glue, such as Super Glue®, or wood glue. Hold the tail in place several moments until the CA glue sets. If you use wood glue, use tape or rubber bands to hold the tail in place until the glue dries.

14 **Refine the tail.** Trim the ends of the tail near the body to smooth the transition between the tail and the body. The tail should taper on the ends until it is flush with the body.

TAIL AND FINS: MAKING THE SIDE FINS

15 **Cut the side fins.** The side fins, which make the lure glide levelly through the water, are cut from sheet copper. Trace around a penny twice to create two circles on the copper sheet. Then, cut the circles using craft scissors.

16 **Refine the side fins.** Cut each copper circle in half to create two side fins. The cutting process may bend the edges of the thin copper. To flatten the edges, clamp the edges of the fins lightly with flat-nose pliers.

TAIL AND FINS: ADD THE SIDE FINS

17 **Carve the grooves for the side fins.** Draw a horizontal line two-thirds to three-quarters of the way down the body on both sides. The lines should start behind the gill and end about ¼" (6mm) from the tail. Stop-cut along the lines and carve up to the stop cuts from a small distance away to create thin grooves.

18 **Position the fins in the grooves.** Slide the copper fins into place inside the thin grooves carved in Step 17. Position the fins anywhere along the groove, but make sure to position them symmetrically on both sides of the lure.

19 **Lock the fins in place.** Run a thin bead of CA glue along the bottom of the copper fins. Allow some of the glue to flow into the groove.

TIPS SCISSOR CARE

Woodcarving can be hazardous to sharp fabric-cutting scissors. In this project we will cut paper, paper bags, cardboard, sandpaper, and copper sheeting with scissors. All of these materials will damage or destroy sharp cutting edges. I keep several pairs of inexpensive or heavily used scissors in my carving kit specifically for this type of use.

I keep my sharp fabric scissors far away from my carving tools.

CHAPTER 4

Creating the Copper Hardware and Stand

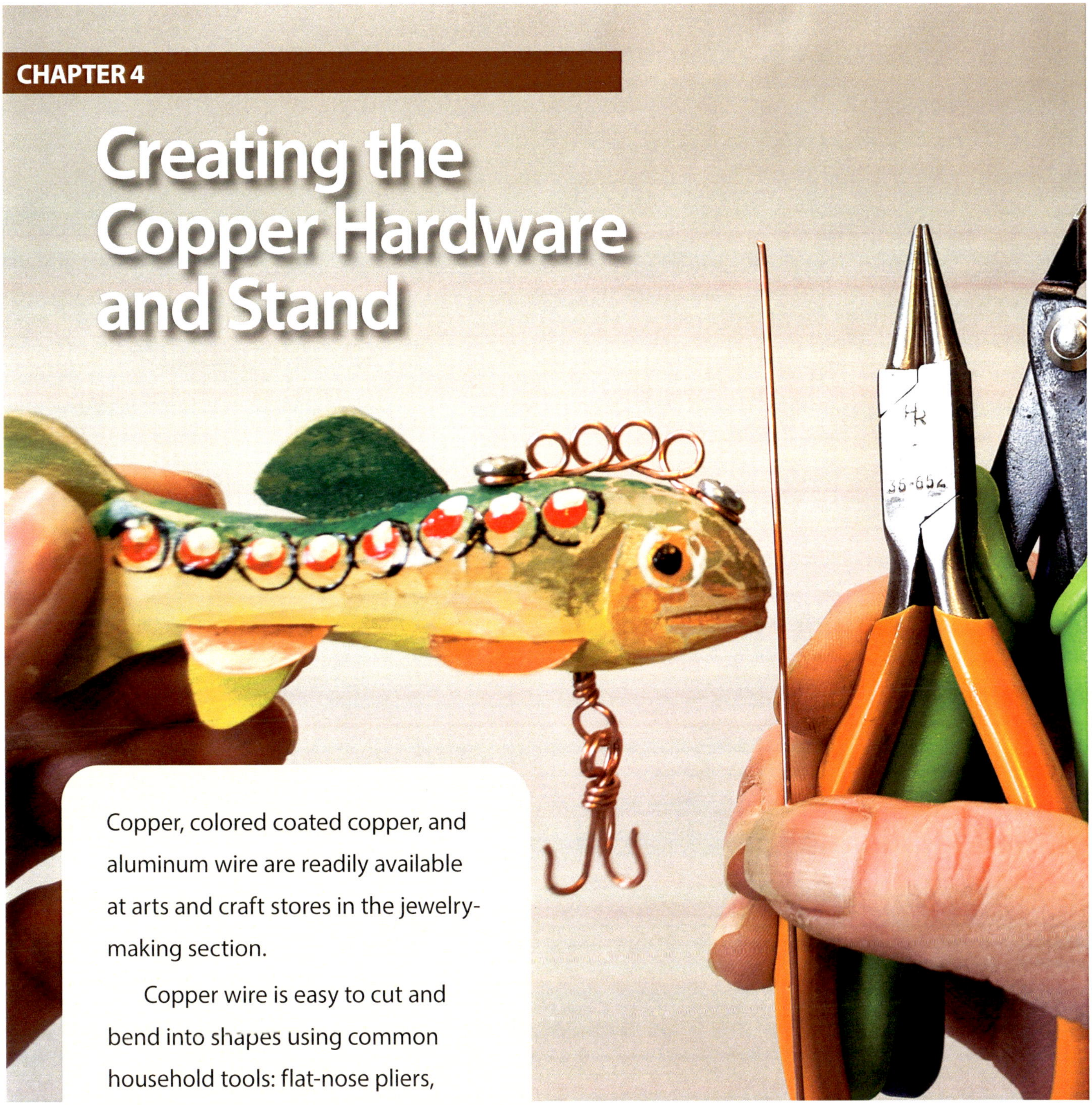

Copper, colored coated copper, and aluminum wire are readily available at arts and craft stores in the jewelry-making section.

Copper wire is easy to cut and bend into shapes using common household tools: flat-nose pliers, round-nose pliers, and wire cutters. Use the wire to make fishing hooks, a display stand, and a line loop to hold the fishing line. For the line loops and hooks, use 18-gauge wire, which is considered a medium thickness of wire. Use heavier and thicker 12-gauge wire for the display stand.

HARDWARE: MAKING THE LINE LOOPS

1 **Create the first circle in the line loops.** Cut a 6" (152mm)-long piece of 18-gauge wire. Using the round-nose pliers, grip the wire in the center. Wrap both ends of the wire around the round-nose pliers to create a circle. Remove the wire from the pliers.

2 **Create the second circle.** With the pliers, grip the wire about 1⁄16" (2mm) in front of the circle made in Step 1. Grip the wire with the same part of the pliers to make the circles the same size. Roll the long end of the wire around the round-nose pliers to create the second circle.

3 **Create the last circle.** Grip the wire in the round-nose pliers about 1⁄16" (2mm) away from the opposite side of the first loop. Again, use the same spot on the pliers to create the same size of circle. Using the technique explained in Step 2, make the third loop. Make sure all three loops are wrapped in the same direction.

HARDWARE: REFINING THE LINE LOOPS

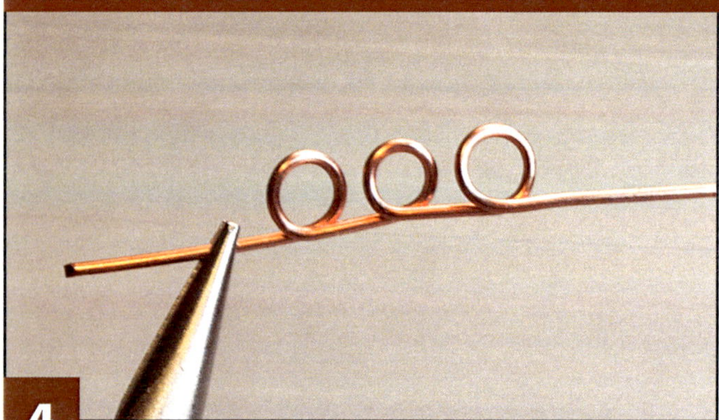

4 **Refine the loops.** Straighten the loops and end wires so you have a straight line along the bottom edge of the line-loops piece.

5 **Begin making the end loops.** The end loops are used to screw the piece to the lure. Use flat-nose pliers to make a 90° bend on the end of the wire near the last loop. The bend makes the wire stick out to the side in relation to the loops.

6 **Create the end loop.** With the tip of the round-nose pliers, grip the wire at the bend. Roll the wire around the pliers, creating a small circle that is centered on the main wire and perpendicular to the three line loops. Repeat Steps 5 and 6 to create the other end loop.

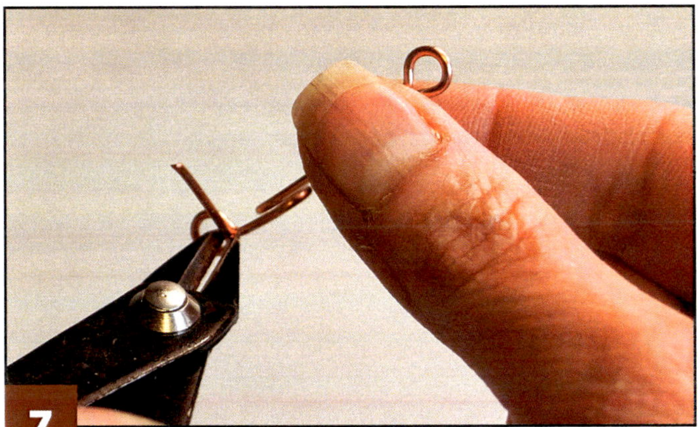

7 **Cut off the excess wire.** Use wire cutters to clip off the wire from the end loops where the excess wire crosses the circles. Flatten the circles by applying gentle pressure with flat-nose pliers.

8 **Test-fit the wire loop.** Position the line-loops piece along the back of the lure and bend it slightly to fit the shape of the lure. Then, set the line loops aside for now.

HARDWARE: MAKING THE HOOK LOOPS

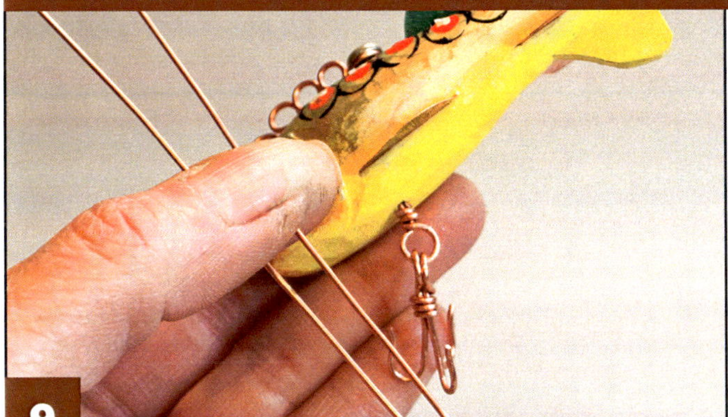

9 **Decide what kind of fishhooks to use.** Purchase pre-made hooks at your local sporting goods store or make your own decorative hooks. I make three-pronged fishhooks.

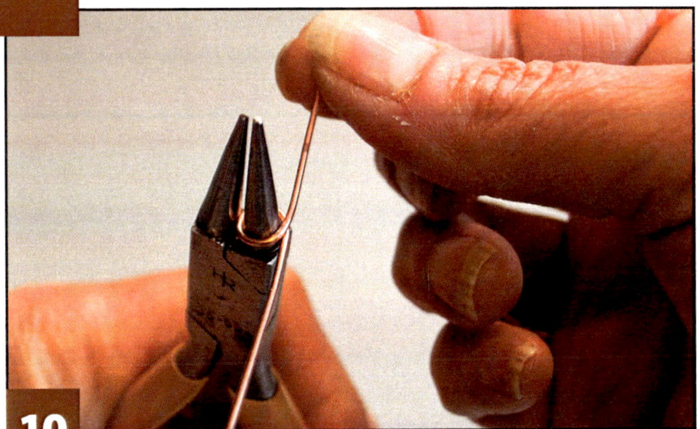

10 **Make a loop.** Cut a 6" (152mm)-long piece of 18-gauge wire. Grip the wire in the center with round-nose pliers. Roll both ends of the wire around the pliers to make a full circle.

HARDWARE: MAKING THE HOOK LOOPS

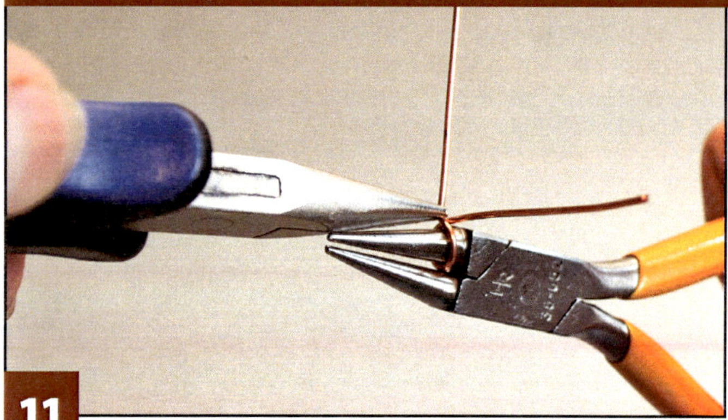

11 **Finish the loop.** Hold the circle securely with the round-nose pliers while you use the flat-nose pliers to create a 90° bend in one leg of the wire at the base of the circle. Bring this leg into a straight upright position bent away from the circle area. Repeat this step on the other end of the wire. Set this loop aside.

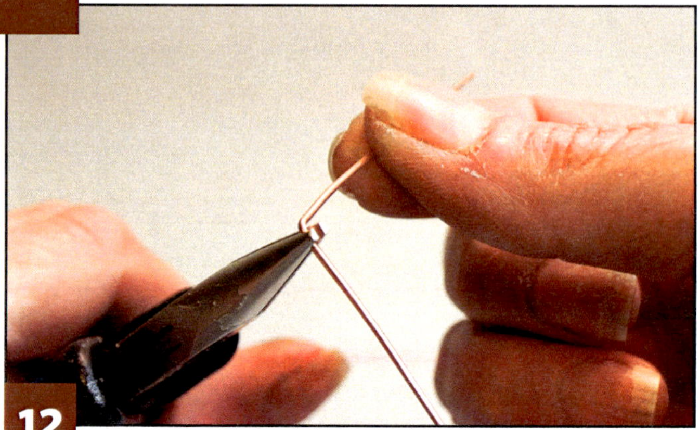

12 **Begin creating the second loop.** Cut a second 6" (152mm)-long piece of 18-gauge wire. With the flat-nose pliers, grip the wire about 3" (76mm) from one end and create a 90° bend in the wire.

13 **Finish the second loop.** Grip the 90° bend in your round-nose pliers and roll the wire into a full circle until the end of the wire is aligned with the 90° bend.

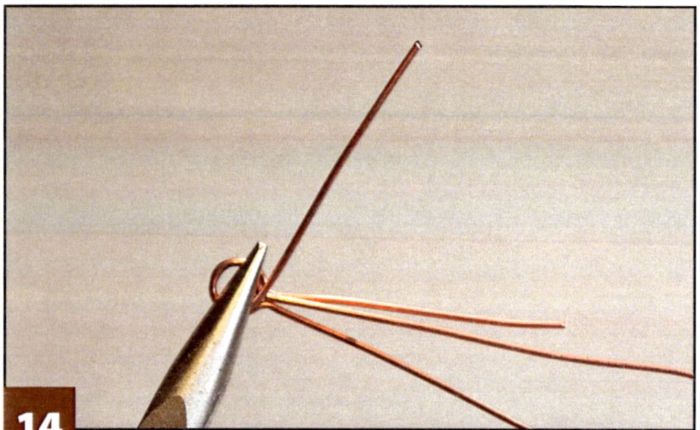

14 **Prepare to wrap the wires together.** Align the circles of both wires. Grip both circles with the flat-nose pliers.

15 **Wrap one wire around the others.** Use your fingers to roll the end of the second wire with the 90° bend around the other three wires (the two ends of the first wire and the remaining end of the second wire). Wrap the wire two to four times around the other three and snip off the excess with wire cutters. Press the cut end of the wire into place alongside the rolls of wire.

HARDWARE: MAKING THE HOOKS

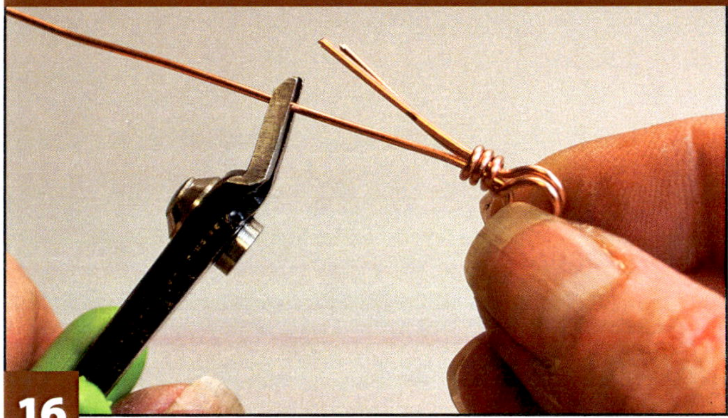

16 **Cut the hook wires to length.** Clip the wires that will become the three hooks down to 1" (25mm) to 1¼" (32mm) long. The length of these wires determines the size of the hooks.

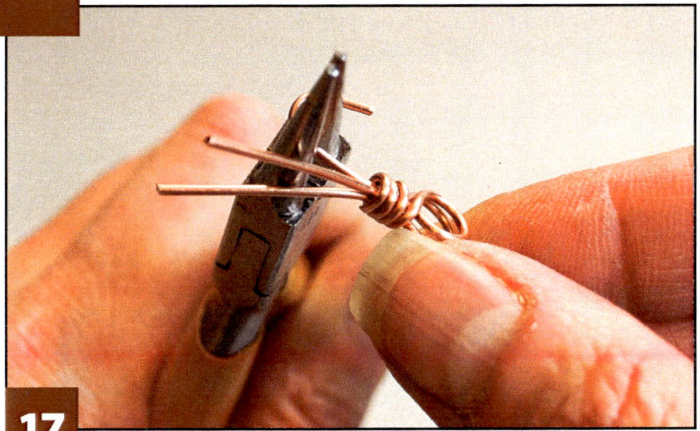

17 **Create the hooks.** With round-nose pliers, grip one hook wire in the center. Roll the wire in a half circle with the end facing outward from the center of the hook. Then, grip the end of the wire with the tip of the round-nose pliers and roll a small half circle onto the wire. Repeat the process on the other two hooks. Set the hook aside.

HARDWARE: MAKING THE HANGING LOOP

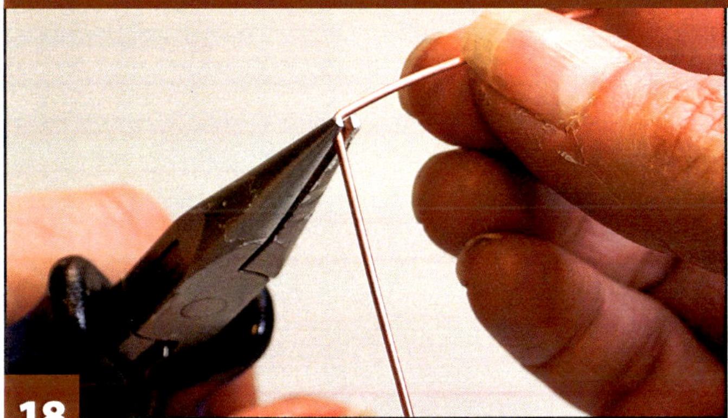

18 **Begin creating the straight hanging loop.** I use a wrapped straight hanging loop to secure the hook to the lure's body. Cut a 6" (152mm)-long piece of 18-gauge wire. With flat-nose pliers, hold the wire 2" to 3" (51mm to 76mm) from one end and create a 90° bend.

19 **Create the circle.** With round-nose pliers, grip the wire at the 90° bend. Roll the wire around to create a full circle. The end of the wire should be at a right angle to the other end of the wire.

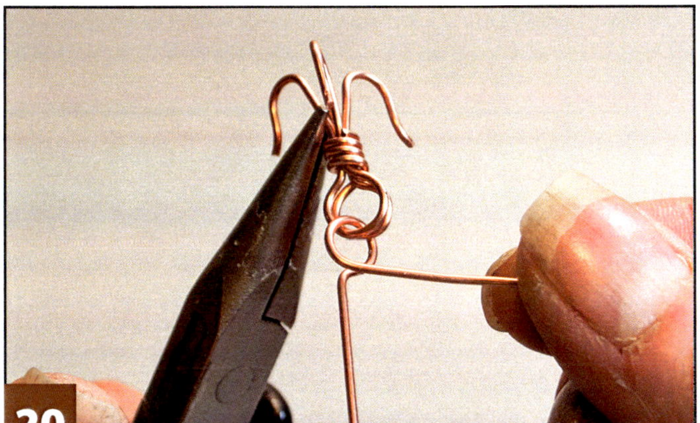

20 **Attach the fishhook to the circle.** Slide the two loops of the fishhook into the circle you made in Step 19.

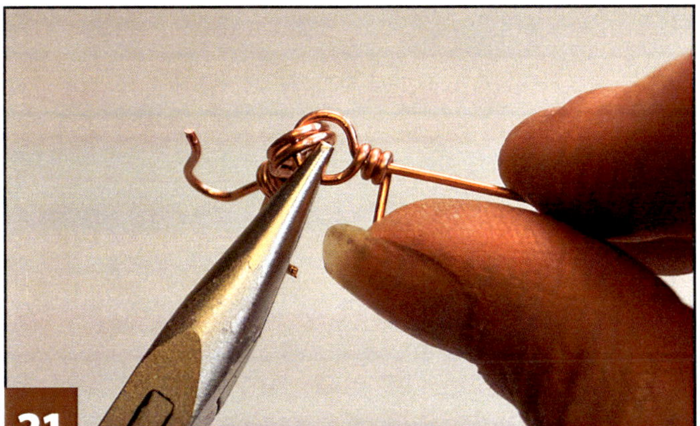

21 **Wrap the wire.** Grip the hanging loop with the flat-nose pliers. Wrap the end with the 90° bend around the other end two to four times. This closes the circle and locks the fish hook circles within the hanging loop.

22 **Cut off the excess wire.** Using wire cutters, clip off the excess wrapped wire; use flat-nose pliers to flatten the cut end into the wrap. Measure ¼" to ⅜" (6mm to 10mm) from the base of the circle and cut off the other end of the wire. Follow Steps 9 through 22 to make another set of hooks and a hanging loop. Set the hooks and loops aside.

HARDWARE: MAKING THE STAND

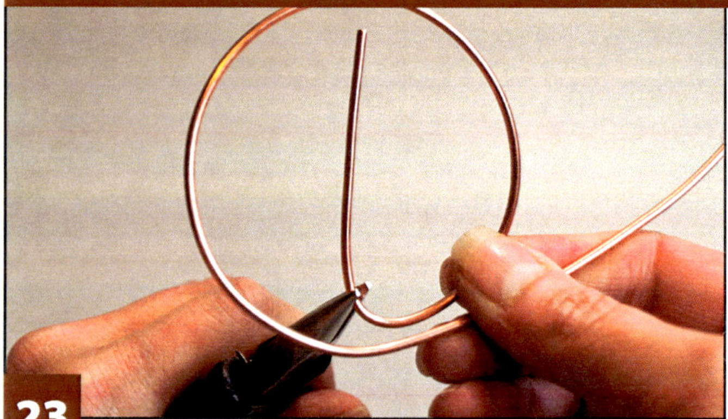

23 **Make the stand base.** Cut an 18" (457mm) length of 12-gauge copper wire. Place the wire against the side of a 2" (51mm)-diameter jar with about 2" (51mm) of wire extending past the side of the jar. Roll the long end of the wire around the jar once, returning to the starting point. Slide the wire circle off the jar. Bend the short overhang at a 90° angle so it sits inside the circle; if the short piece extends beyond the circle, cut it off.

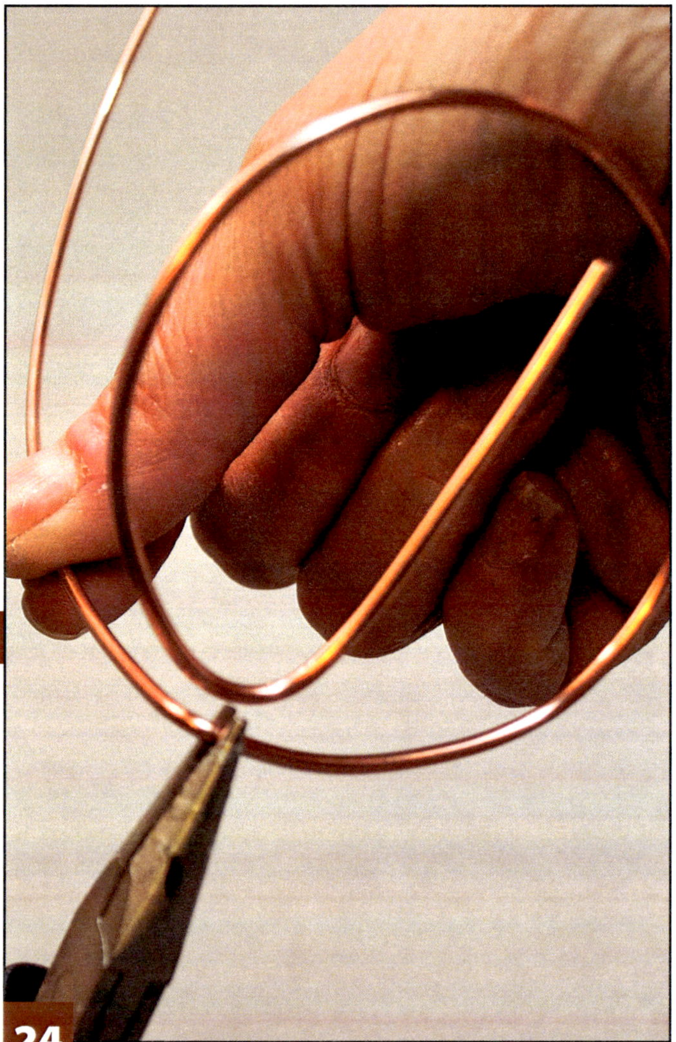

24 **Create the upright arm.** Use flat-nose pliers to grip the long wire end where the circle closes; bend the wire upward at a right angle. Cut the upright off about 6" (152mm) from the circle base.

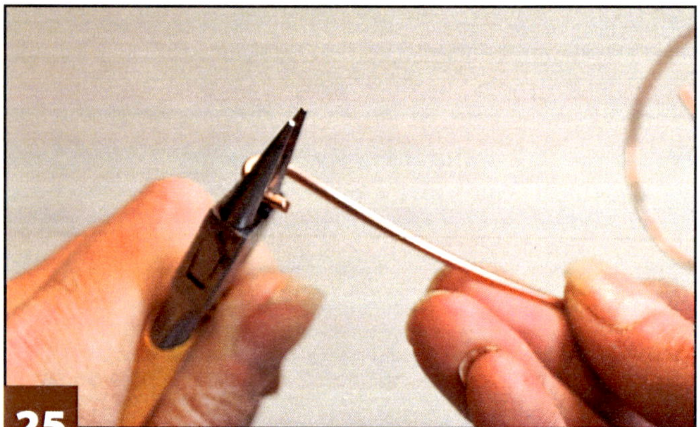

25 **Shape the hook.** Grip the end of the wire with round-nose pliers and bend the wire into a half circle that turns away from the base loop toward the back of the display.

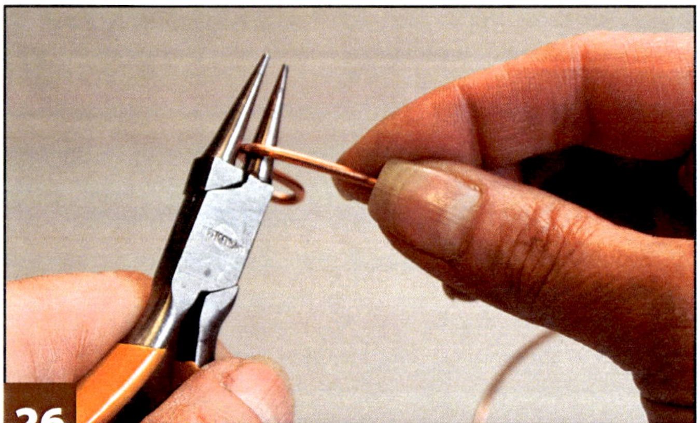

26 **Finish the display.** Using round-nose pliers, grasp the wire about ¾" (19mm) from the end loop and bend it forward to form a loose S. Use your fingers to arc the upright so the hook points upward and is positioned roughly over the front of the base circle.

CHAPTER 5

Painting the Lure and Attaching the Hardware

While it's possible to apply a simple oil finish or clear coat of lacquer to the lure, it will look more authentic if you paint it. You don't need expensive paints, thinners, or airbrushes—all you need are some acrylic craft paints, a few paintbrushes, and a pencil.

Before we begin these painting steps, let's return to my great-grandfather for a few moments. He spent his entire adult life working in a coal mine. I expect his hands were coarse, callused, and perhaps even arthritic. I doubt he would have had any art training, let alone fine art painting. If you asked him about doing an art project, he would have told you he "couldn't draw a straight line even if you gave him a ruler."

Few whittlers in the heyday of the fish lure were trained artists. They were not concerned about painting their lures in a realistic or detailed way. Fishing lure coloring is used to deceive the predator fish by giving an impression of coloring, stripe patterns, or spotting that would be found on a minnow.

I don't think any large-mouth bass ever rejected a homemade fishing lure because the paint lines weren't straight. So if you have not used a paintbrush before, do not be concerned. By the time you have worked through these steps, you will have a wonderfully colored vintage look to your lure.

Basswood, with its clear white grain, is an excellent wood for painted projects. I use artist-quality acrylic paint. You can also use acrylic craft paints or markers. Most painted carvings begin with a primer coat of white, medium gray, or black.

PAINTING: APPLYING THE BASE COATS

1 **Apply a base coat.** Apply one to two thin coats of black paint to the entire carving. As you work, smooth any brush-stroke ridges by working over those areas with a clean brush. Around the copper fins, use a marker to insure a straight even coloring layer. Allow the base coat to dry for thirty minutes.

2 **Paint the bottom half of the lure.** Mix half a brushful of burnt sienna with a quarter-sized puddle of titanium white. Apply two coats of this reddish-white mixture to the belly, bottom fin, bottom of the face, and the gill areas. Some of the black base coat will show through the reddish-white color.

3 **Paint the rest of the body.** Add a small amount of medium green to the mixture made in Step 2. Stir the new mixture lightly, but allow the paint puddle to have variations in color. Apply two light coats of the new mixture to the top half of the lure's body.

4 **Paint the top of the lure.** Mix together equal parts burnt sienna and medium green to make a dark greenish-brown. Apply two coats of this mixture to the top third of the body, the top fin, and the tail.

5 **Check your progress.** Notice I have not created a straight line or an even coating during any of these painting steps. Set the lure aside to dry thoroughly for thirty minutes.

PAINTING: ADDING THE DOTS

6 **Prepare to add the yellow spots.** Place some pale yellow paint on the palette and pull the color into a flat thin layer with a brush. To get regular-sized spots, dip an unused pencil eraser into the paint. Make sure you cover the entire surface of the eraser.

7 **Apply the yellow spots.** Make a series of dots by touching the paint-covered eraser in a line down the back of the lure. Make one line along each side, running from just behind the gill to the tail. Make one to two spots for each eraser dip into the paint.

8 **Add the eyes.** Wipe the eraser clean on a dry paper towel. Using the technique explained in Steps 6 and 7, dip the eraser in titanium white paint and dot eyes on both sides of the face.

9 **Prepare to add the small dots.** To create the small red and black spots, cut the graphite end off of a pencil with a knife and smooth the end with 220-grit sandpaper.

10 **Add the small dots.** Use the same process explained in Steps 6 and 7, but use the graphite end of the pencil you modified in Step 9. Add a row of small red spots under each row of yellow spots. Then, add black dots in the center of the white eyes. Allow the paint to dry overnight.

PAINTING: ADDING THE FINAL DETAILS

11 **Distress the lure.** Gently rub the lure with 220-grit sandpaper, removing some of the top layers of paint. This reveals the black base coat and some raw wood. The spot colors may be dragged into other areas by the sanding process; this increases the vintage effect.

12 **Add scales to the bottom.** To catch the predator fish's attention, add metallic gold or silver scales to the belly area using a permanent marker.

FINISHING: ATTACHING THE LINE LOOPS

13 **Prepare to add the line loops.** Hold the line loops in position and use a marker to mark the location of the screw loops.

14 **Drill the pilot holes.** Drill 1⁄16"-diameter by ¼"-deep (2mm by 6mm) pilot holes at the marks made in Step 13.

15 **Attach the line loops.** Hold the line loops in position and drive a ¼" (6mm)-long screw into each hole.

Mismatched Hardware

When my husband looked over my carved lures, he noted I used Phillips-head steel screws to set the loop line of my spotted minnow lure. He said he doubted my great-grandfather would have had Phillips-head screws. My reply was that my great-grandfather would have used whatever was at hand. So, in the time-honored tradition of lure carving, I rummaged through my jar of loose screws and used whatever I found.

FINISHING: ATTACHING THE HOOKS

16 **Drill the pilot holes for the hooks.** Drill a 1⁄16"-diameter by 1⁄4"-deep (2mm by 6mm) pilot hole centered between each pair of copper fins.

17 **Attach the hooks.** Add a drop of CA glue to the pilot hole and push the shank of the straight hanging loop into the hole. Add a second drop of CA glue at the bottom of the loop. Hold the loop a few seconds with the flat-nose pliers until the glue sets. Use the same process to attach the other hook assembly.

18 **Seal the carving.** Add a few more dots of color with a red marking pen if desired. Then, seal the lure with several light coats of high-gloss acrylic spray sealer, following the manufacturer's instructions.

CHAPTER 6

Making a Homemade Bobber

No lure would be complete without a bobber. To catch enough fish for a meal, my great-grandfather often had two or three lines in the water at the same time. Wooden bobbers made it easy to see at a glance which lines had fish biting.

This homemade bobber makes a nice decorative accent for a carved fishing lure display.

TIPS **STAINING THE CORD**

As I was working on the bobber, I realized my cord, mason's line, was pure white and stuck out like a sore thumb against my vintage lure. To darken the cord, I soaked it in coffee for a half-hour. You could also darken it by dragging it through well-thinned brown paint.

BOBBER: ROUGHING OUT THE PROJECT

1 Mark the center of the blank. Cut the blank to size and draw a pencil line from corner to corner on both ends of the blank. Where the two lines cross is the center of the blank.

2 Drill a hole through the blank. Drill a ¼" (6mm)-diameter hole through the blank. The slightly oversized hole makes it easy to insert and adjust the position of the dowel.

3 Remove the sharp corners of the blank. Round each side and taper it smoothly to the holes in the two ends.

4 Finish carving the bobber. Continue rounding and tapering the bobber until it is shaped like an elongated egg.

BOBBER: ASSEMBLING THE PROJECT

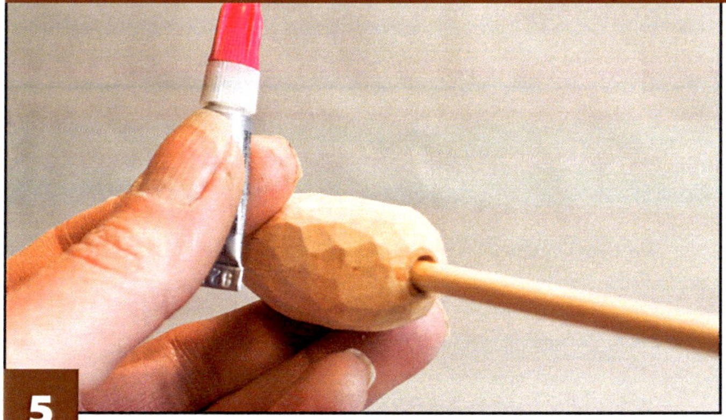

5 Glue the dowel in place. Slide a 3⁄16" (5mm)-diameter dowel through the hole. Make sure an equal length of dowel sticks out both ends of the bobber. Then, lock the dowel in place with CA glue or wood glue. Allow the glue to dry.

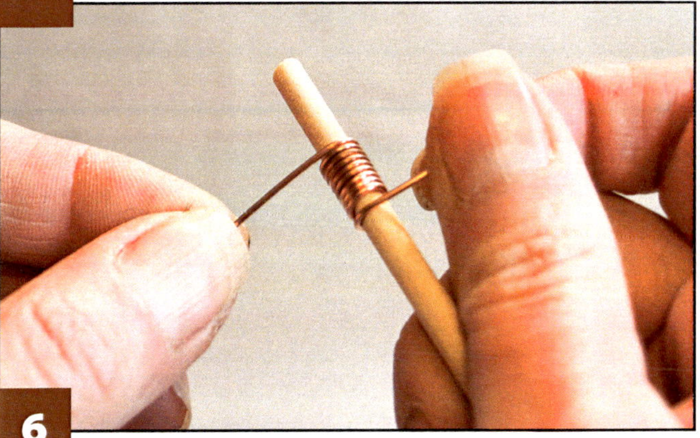

6 Begin making the end coils. Cut an 18" (457mm)-long piece of 18-gauge wire. Wrap the wire tightly around an end of the dowel. The goal is to have ten to twelve tightly compressed coils. Repeat the process on the other end of the dowel with another piece of wire.

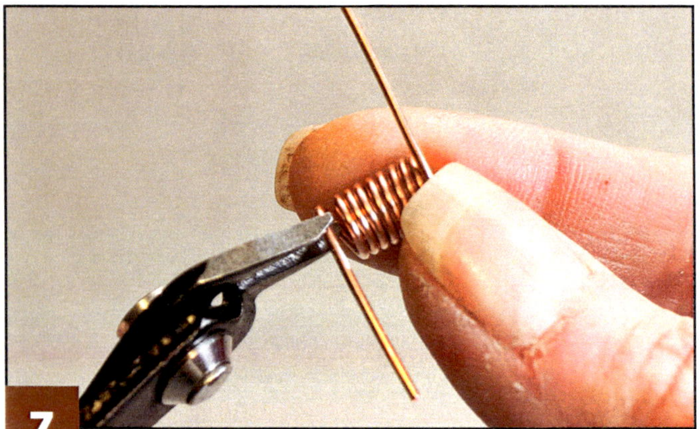

7 **Remove the coils from the dowel.** Slide the coils off the dowel and clip off the excess wire from the ends using wire cutters..

8 **Finish the coils.** Use wire cutters or a bench knife to gently open the space between the second and third coil on the roll. Bend the first two or three coils up so they sit at a 90° angle to the rest of the roll. Repeat for the second coil.

BOBBER: FINISHING THE PROJECT

9 **Paint the bobber.** Use a pencil to divide the bobber in half. Apply one to two coats of bright red acrylic paint to one half of the bobber, stopping at the centerline. Paint the other half of the bobber with one to two coats of white acrylic paint. Allow the paint to dry thoroughly, and then distress it using the techniques explained on page 30 (Step 11 of Chapter 5). Remove any sanding dust with a dry lint-free cloth.

10 **Attach the copper hardware.** Slide a copper coil onto each end of the bobber dowel. The first two rings of the coil should stick out from the end of the dowel. Lock the coils in place with CA glue. Allow the glue to dry, and then seal the carving with two or three light coats of high-gloss acrylic spray sealer.

11 **Add the cord.** Cut a 15" (381mm)-long piece of mason's line or heavy cord. Thread the cord through one copper coil and tie with an overhand knot. Bring the cord to the opposite end of the bobber, thread it through the coil, and tie with an overhand knot. Allow some slack in the cord between the two ends of the bobber.

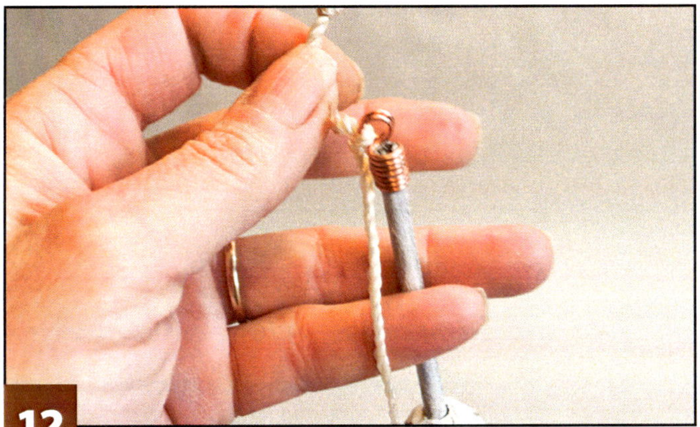

12 **Cut off the excess cord.** Tie an overhand knot in the cord on the white side of the bobber 1" to 1½" (25mm to 51mm) from the coil. Cut the excess cord about 1" (25mm) from the knot and fray the end with your fingers.

13 **Attach the bobber to the lure.** Thread the remaining long end of bobber cord through the line loops on the lure and tie the end to one of the loops.

Lures don't have to resemble fish. Create a lure shaped like a mouse or a turtle. Use the completed lures as decorative accents on signs.

The pattern for the gar fishing lure carved in the demonstration is on page 15. All other patterns are on pages 37 through 40.

Folk-art fishing lures can be used to embellish picture frames or other projects.

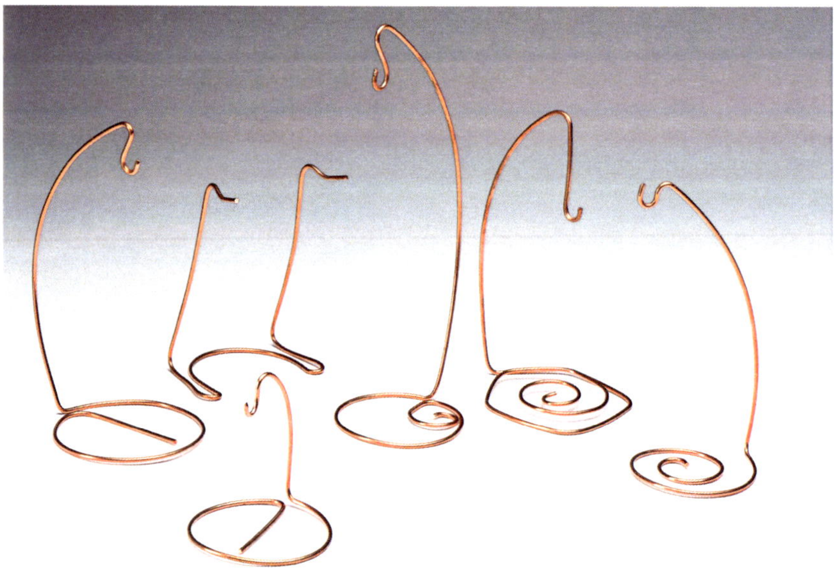

Create different stands for your lures by making simple alterations to the basic design.

Largemouth bass pattern

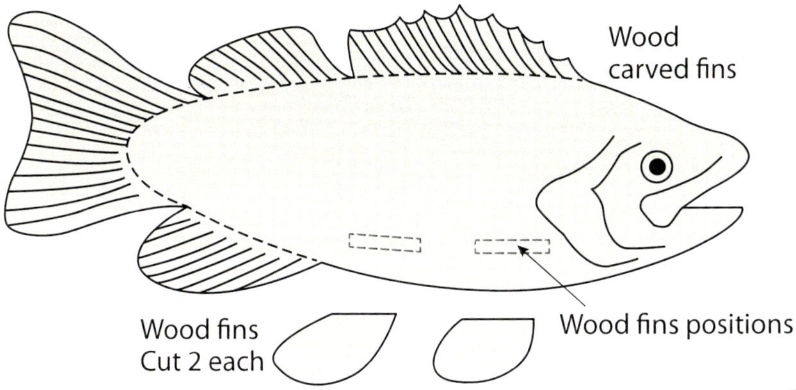

Blue gill pattern

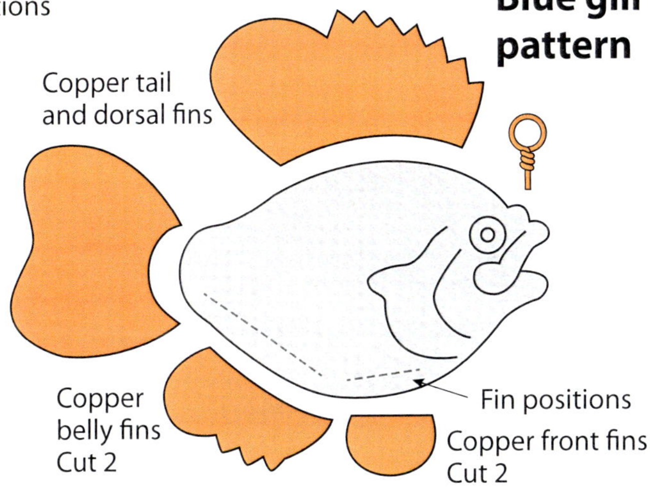

Speckled minnow pattern

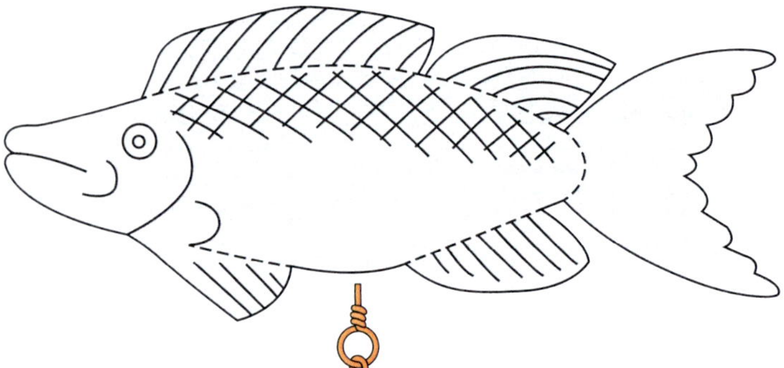

Spotted minnow pattern

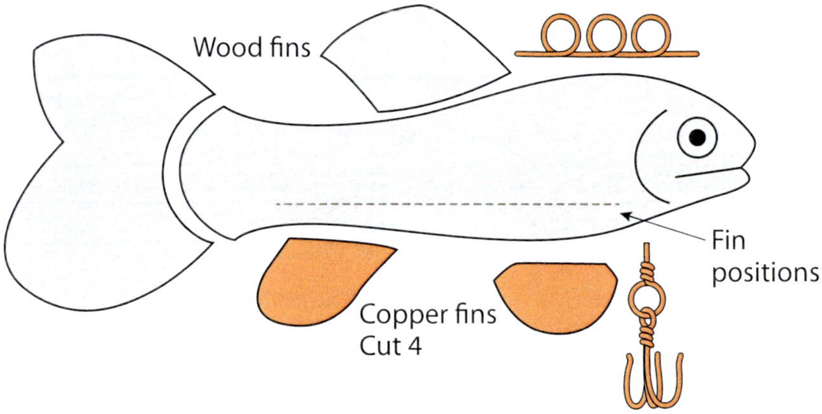

Red salmon pattern

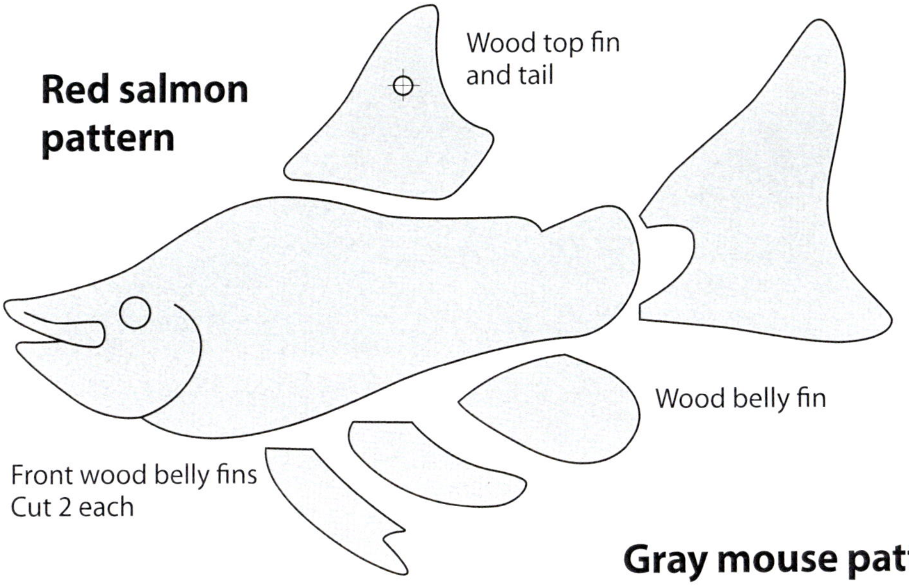

Gray mouse pattern

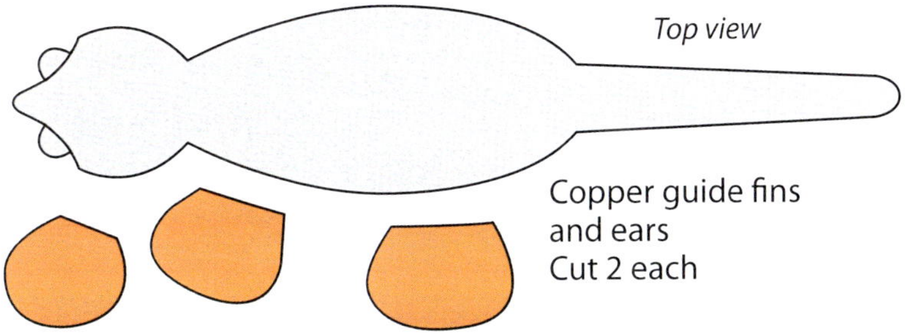

Sunny pattern

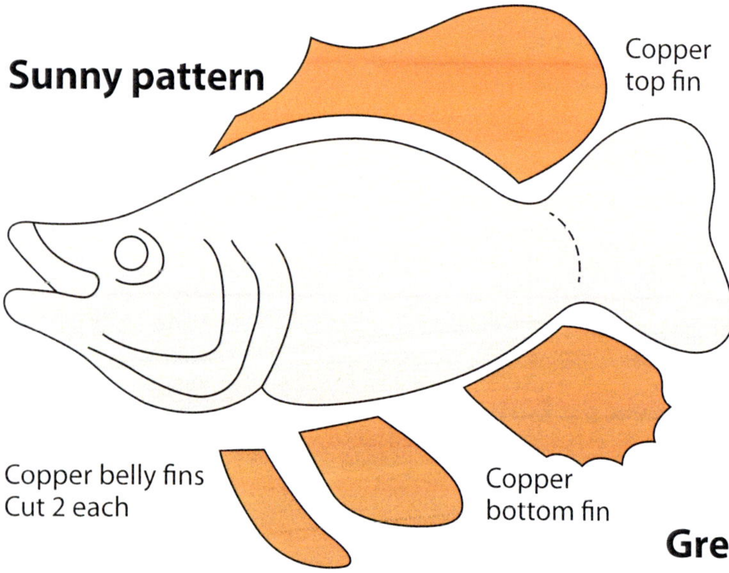

Green gar pattern

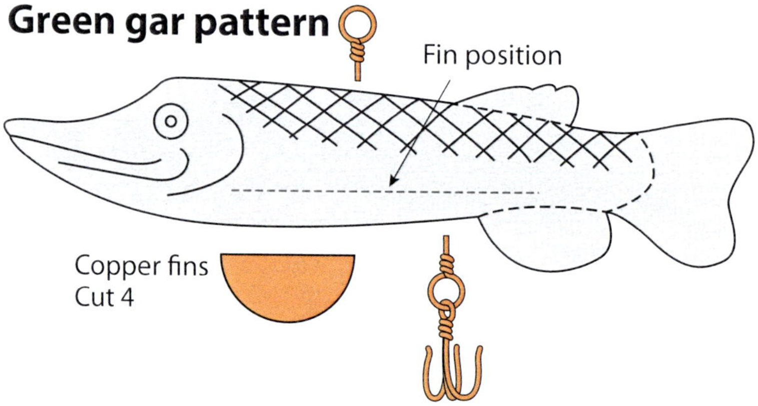